STECK-VAUGHN
SPECIAL
EDITION

SEPTEMBER 11, 2001

STECK-VAUGHN
ELEMENTARY · SECONDARY · ADULT · LIBRARY

A Harcourt Company

www.steck-vaughn.com

Acknowledgments

Editorial Director: Diane Schnell
Associate Editor: Terra G. Tarango
Associate Director of Design: Joyce Spicer
Senior Designer: Joan Cunningham
Production Manager: Mychael Ferris-Pacheco
Production Coordinator: Paula Schumann
Electronic Production Specialist: Scott Melcer
Media Researcher: Nicole Mlakar

Photography: Cover (fireman) ©Brad Rickerby/REUTERS/CORBIS; (TV) ©Shannon Stapleton/REUTERS/TimePix; (Afghanistan) ©ROBERT NICKELSBERG/TimePix; (smoke) ©Jaimie Collins; p.1 ©Jaimie Collins; p.4 ©Sung Park/Austin American-Statesman; p.6 © Ecoscene/CORBIS; p.8 ©Kelley-Mooney/CORBIS; p.11 ©AP/Wide World; p.14 ©ROBERT NICKELSBERG/TimePix; p.16 ©Mian Khursheed/REUTERS/TimePix; p.17 ©Holton Collection/SuperStock; p.18 © Chris Hondros/Getty Images; p.19 ©Farooq Khan/AP/Wide World; p.20 © Pawel Kopczynski/REUTERS/CORBIS; p.21(a) ©Ron Frehm/AP/Wide World; p.21(b) ©Brennan Linsley/AP/Wide World; p. 21(c) ©U.S.Navy/Handout/REUTERS/CORBIS; p.23 ©AP/Wide World; p.26 ©Sgt. David W. Richards/Courtesy of U.S. Air Force; p.29(bg) ©Peter Morgan/REUTERS/CORBIS; p.29(a) ©David Lloyd/Tribune-Democrat/AP/Wide World; p.29(b) ©William Philpott/REUTERS/CORBIS; pp.36-37 ©Mike Segar/REUTERS/CORBIS; p.39 ©Ethan Miller/REUTERS/TimePix; pp.40-41 ©Jaimie Collins; p.48 ©Thomas E. Franklin/The Record/Corbis SABA.

Diagrams and maps: D&G Limited, LLC

ISBN 0-7398-6006-2

Copyright ©2002 Steck-Vaughn Company

Printed in the United States of America

1 2 3 4 5 6 7 8 9 LB 06 05 04 03 02

Contents

On September 11, 2001, four planes were **hijacked** by a group of 19 men. Two planes crashed into the World Trade Center towers in New York City. Both towers **collapsed**. The third plane crashed into the Pentagon in Washington, D.C. The fourth plane crashed in a field in Pennsylvania. Thousands of people were killed.

These attacks led the United States into a "War on **Terrorism**." Within days, the news was about people and places many Americans knew little about—people like Osama bin Laden, places like Afghanistan. Americans suddenly wanted to know more about the buildings that were attacked. They wanted to learn about the people and places that were involved.

This book gives answers to some commonly asked questions. Who worked in the World Trade Center? What is the Taliban? Who is Osama bin Laden? How has America responded to the attacks? This book gives the background information to help understand this eventful day in history. With that background, you may better understand the events that shape our world since September 11, 2001.

CHAPTER 1

Before the Attacks

**The World Trade Center
before September 11, 2001**

The World Trade Center was a group of seven
buildings. The most famous buildings of the World
Trade Center were the two "twin towers." They stood
taller than any other buildings in New York City. They
were built between the years 1966 and 1973. At the
time they were built, they were the tallest buildings

in the world. Tower One was 1,368 feet tall. It had a radio antenna that rose from the roof another 360 feet. Tower Two stood 1,362 feet tall.

Each tower had 110 stories and 104 elevators. Some of the elevators were the size of a classroom. Each floor of the towers was the size of a city block. The towers had 16 miles of stairs. They received so much mail that the towers had their own zip code. From the **observation deck** on the 107th floor of Tower Two, people could see 45 miles in every direction.

Who worked in the World Trade Center?

About 50,000 people worked in the World Trade Center towers. **Financial** companies filled most of the offices. The towers were located in a part of New York City called the Financial District. Most of the companies in this area work with money.

Many of the people who worked in the World Trade Center helped people who put money into the **stock market**. People **invest** money in the stock market in hopes that their money will be worth more later. Companies called **investment firms** help people decide where to put their money. There were more than 50 investment firms in the World Trade Center towers. There were more than 100 banks.

There also were many stores and restaurants in the towers. A fancy restaurant called Windows on the World was located at the top of Tower One. People liked to eat there and enjoy the views of the city.

In addition to all the workers at the World Trade Center, there were many visitors. More than 70,000 people visited the towers each day.

The Windows on the World Restaurant

How was the World Trade Center built?

Very tall buildings are called **skyscrapers**. They are called this because they look like they scrape the top of the sky. If you wanted to build a skyscraper, you would have to think about all the problems a tall building faces. The wind gets stronger the higher you go. Your building would have to be strong enough not to be blown down. The ground below the building moves. With a very tall building this could be dangerous. Your

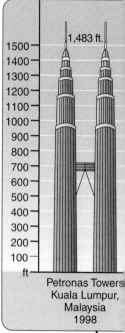

1,483 ft.

1500
1400
1300
1200
1100
1000
900
800
700
600
500
400
300
200
100
ft

Petronas Towers
Kuala Lumpur,
Malaysia
1998

building would have to be built deep enough into the ground that it couldn't move with the ground.

The World Trade Center towers were skyscrapers called tube buildings. The outer walls of the towers were made with columns and beams built very closely together. The columns and beams formed a steel tube around each tower. Inside each tower was one strong column with steel beams running up and down. The steel tube on the outside and the strong column on the inside kept the wind from blowing the towers down. But each tower would **sway** up to three feet from the center with strong winds.

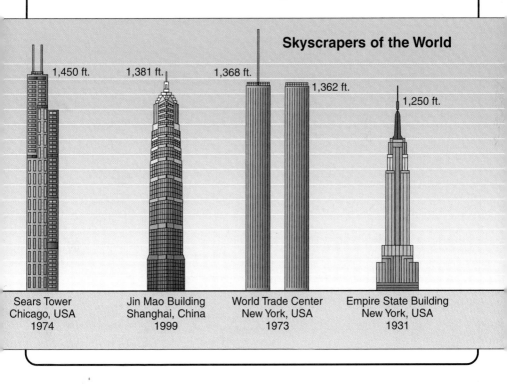

Skyscrapers of the World

| | 1,450 ft. | 1,381 ft. | 1,368 ft. | 1,362 ft. | 1,250 ft. |

| Sears Tower
Chicago, USA
1974 | Jin Mao Building
Shanghai, China
1999 | World Trade Center
New York, USA
1973 | Empire State Building
New York, USA
1931 |

The land below the World Trade Center is actually **landfill**. Landfill is made from trash and other materials. These materials are moved into the ocean or another place to be used as land for more buildings.

Landfill is softer than real ground. So the World Trade Center had to be built more than 70 feet below the ground. Only then did it reach ground hard enough to keep it from sinking. The builders used this underground area for a shopping mall and a subway station.

Was the World Trade Center attacked before September 11, 2001?

In 1993 a bomb went off in the garage of the World Trade Center. Six people were killed and more than one thousand were **injured**. A teacher had taken her class to visit the towers on a field trip that day. The teacher and seventeen children were stuck in an elevator for five hours. None of them were hurt.

What is the Pentagon?

The Pentagon is the main office building of the Department of Defense. It is located in Washington, D.C. It is where most of the country's **military** leaders

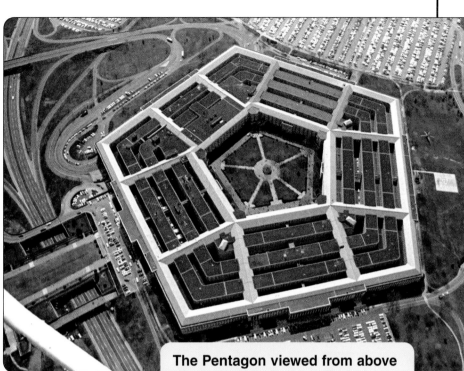

The Pentagon viewed from above before September 11, 2001

work to defend the country. The Pentagon is really like a small city. More than 20,000 people work there. It has its own cafeterias, libraries, and even a post office.

The name of this building comes from its unusual shape. A **pentagon** is a five-sided shape. The Pentagon building is actually five pentagons, called rings. Each ring is built outside another. When viewed from above, the Pentagon almost looks like a maze.

How big is the Pentagon?

The Pentagon is one of the largest office spaces in the world. It is only five stories high, but it has miles of floor space. Find the Empire State Building on the chart on page 9. Even though New York City's Empire State Building is 102 stories tall, the Pentagon has three times the floor space of the Empire State Building.

A building as big as the Pentagon must be well designed. It must be easy to get from one part of the building to another. It also must be strong enough to hold the weight of the building, all its furniture, and all its people.

The Pentagon was built in 1943, and it is still thought of as one of the best-designed office buildings in the world. How long do you think it would take to walk from one side of the Pentagon to the other? Even with more than 17 miles of hallways, it takes only seven minutes to walk between any two points on opposite sides of the building.

CHAPTER 2

Afghanistan

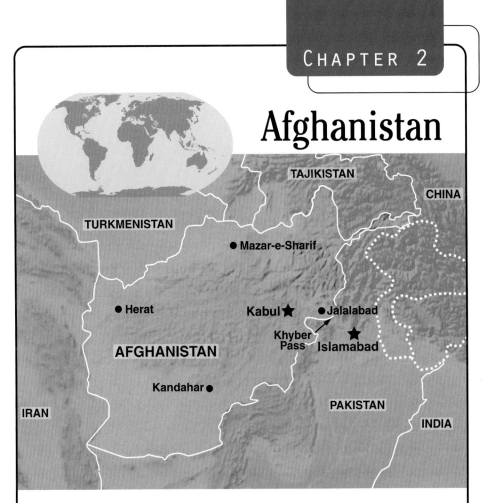

Afghanistan is located in a part of the world where many different people come together. To the west of Afghanistan are Iran and the Middle East, and east of Afghanistan is China. North of Afghanistan are Russia and some smaller countries that used to be part of the Soviet Union. To the southeast are Pakistan and India. Each of these areas has different groups of people with different languages and **religions**.

The rugged land
of Afghanistan

Afghanistan is home to 26 million people from many different groups. They live on land that is rough and **rugged**. Parts of the country are more than four miles high. Tall mountains and dry deserts make it difficult to travel across the country. The winters are very cold. The summers are hot and dry.

What's the history of Afghanistan?

Many people have fought over and ruled the land now called Afghanistan. Powerful groups such as the Persians, the Greeks, and the Mongols ruled this region at one time or another. In the early 1800s, Great Britain and Russia fought for control of the land. Russia wanted to gain land connecting it with the Indian Ocean. Great Britain controlled India and wanted to protect it. Great Britain gained some control over Afghanistan.

In 1919 Afghanistan became an **independent** country. It was free from Great Britain. Still, different groups within the country fought for control.

Russia joined with other countries and became the Soviet Union. In 1979, the Soviet Union **invaded** Afghanistan. The war lasted for ten years. The Soviets had stronger weapons, but the Afghans won the war. They knew the land better than the Soviets, and they were fighting to keep their home. The United States helped Afghanistan fight against the Soviet Union.

What is the Taliban?

After the Soviets left Afghanistan, the fighting among different groups continued. Governments came and went until one group took control in 1996. This group was the Taliban.

A Taliban soldier

At first, the Afghan people welcomed the Taliban. They brought peace to a country that had been fighting for 20 years. The Taliban brought peace by making **strict** rules for the people. But these rules soon hurt the people. Many Afghan people became afraid of the Taliban. The United Nations, a group of nearly 200 countries around the world, never recognized the Taliban as the real government of Afghanistan.

The Taliban made the strict rules because of their religion, Islam. They wanted to create a country with the most pure form of Islam. But other people who practice Islam do not believe in making such strict rules.

What is Islam?

Most Afghans believe in Islam. Islam is one of three major religions that believe in one God. Judaism is the oldest of these religions. Followers of Judaism are called Jews. Abraham is one of the most important people in their religion. Another religion is Christianity. People who believe in Christianity are called Christians. They follow the teachings of Jesus.

A place where
Afghan Muslims pray

Islam also teaches about one God. People who practice the religion of Islam are called Muslims. Muslims believe in Allah, which is the Arabic word for "God." They believe both Abraham and Jesus were important people. But a man named Muhammad is the most important person in Islam. Muhammad was born in Arabia in the year 570. Muslims believe Muhammad was a messenger of Allah. They believe Allah told Muhammad about how people should live. They also believe Muhammad wrote what Allah told him in a book called the **Koran**.

Muslims praying

For many Muslims, Islam is a way of life. The Koran teaches Muslims to pray five times a day. So, throughout the day Muslims are reminded to obey Allah and live in a peaceful way. Most Muslims believe the Koran teaches peace.

A small group of Muslims think the Koran teaches war. These people are called **Islamic extremists**. Islamic extremists make up a very small number of all Muslims. Members of the Taliban are Islamic extremists. They think countries like the United States are evil. They don't like the way Americans run their government, the way Americans dress, or the kinds of movies Americans watch.

What is life like in Afghanistan?

Life is very hard for many Afghans. Imagine waking up to a bug crawling across your face. The rock you used as a pillow has scratched the side of your cheek. Your stomach growls from hunger. You know that all you will have to eat is a piece of moldy bread that your mother bought a few days ago. Moldy

Many Afghan children do not have enough to eat.

bread is sold for animals, but it is all your mother could afford. You'll have to share that piece of bread with your brother and sister. Sadly, this is how many children wake up every morning in Afghanistan.

Twenty years of war has been hard on the Afghan people. Many people have been killed in war. Fighting for that long has left little time for people to go to school, build businesses, or earn money. Most Afghans are very poor. Most Afghans cannot read. Many people do not have warm clothing, housing, or medical care.

Afghan women had to cover their faces.

There also has been a **drought** since the late 1990s. Very little rain has fallen in all that time. Without rain, the people cannot grow enough food to eat.

Life is not easy for the Afghan people. But it is even harder for women. The Taliban government made rules that treated women differently than men. Most Americans think the way the Taliban treated women was unfair. Under the Taliban, women could not show any part of their skin, not even their face. Women in Afghanistan were once doctors and teachers. After the Taliban took over, they were not allowed to work or even go to school. If they were caught breaking the rules, they were **severely** punished.

The Taliban also made rules against **entertainment**. People were not allowed to listen to music or watch movies. If a person was caught listening to music, the Taliban punished the person. They would even take music tape and tie it around trees. They did this to warn other Afghan people not to break the law.

CHAPTER 3

Terrorism

Terrorism can hurt people and destroy property.

Left: World Trade Center, 1993
Top Right: African Embassy, 1998
Bottom Right: USS *Cole*, 2000

The word "terrorism" has been used for more than 200 years. It began in France at a time known as the "Reign of Terror." During this time, the leaders of France tried to kill people who were against the French government. Since then, terrorism has been used to describe any time a person or a group tries to scare another person or group into changing the way they think. The people who bomb buildings or hijack planes are known as **terrorists**.

There are terrorist groups around the world. Some areas have more terrorism than others. Northern Ireland and the Middle East are two regions where terrorism is very common. In the Middle East there are even training camps that teach terrorism. One of these camps is named Al Qaeda and is located in Afghanistan.

What is Al Qaeda?

Al Qaeda was started in 1988 by a man named Osama bin Laden. Al Qaeda is an Arabic word which means, "The Camp." The terrorist training camp was started to give money and weapons to the Afghan people fighting against the Soviets. After Afghanistan won the war against the Soviets, Al Qaeda had a new purpose. Many Islamic extremists in Al Qaeda were angry with the United States. The new goal of Al Qaeda became carrying out terrorist attacks that would hurt the United States.

The men in Al Qaeda learn to use weapons and plan terrorist attacks. Some train to be **suicide bombers**. Suicide bombers are willing to kill themselves in order to kill large numbers of their enemy. The men in Al Qaeda believe the Koran tells them to fight a war against countries like the United States. Because they think Allah is telling them to fight the war, they are willing to die for their beliefs. They are also very loyal to their leader, Osama bin Laden.

Osama bin Laden

Who is Osama bin Laden?

Osama bin Laden was born in Riyadh, Saudi Arabia, in 1957. He was one of around 50 children. He had many brothers and sisters because his father had several wives. Osama bin Laden's father had started a **construction** business and had become very rich. Before long, the bin Laden family was one of the richest in Saudi Arabia. Osama bin Laden's father died in a plane crash when Osama was only a child.

Osama bin Laden finished school in 1979, the same year that the Soviet Union invaded Afghanistan. Bin Laden was angry about the war. He wanted to defend the Muslims of Afghanistan against the powerful Soviet Union. At the age of 22, he left Saudi Arabia to help Afghanistan. In 1989, the Soviets finally left Afghanistan, and bin Laden returned to Saudi Arabia.

Osama bin Laden was considered a hero for helping Afghanistan. But then the government forced him to stay inside Saudi Arabia.

Osama bin Laden's life changed greatly in 1990. In that year Iraq invaded the small nation of Kuwait, which is next to Saudi Arabia. Saudi Arabia was

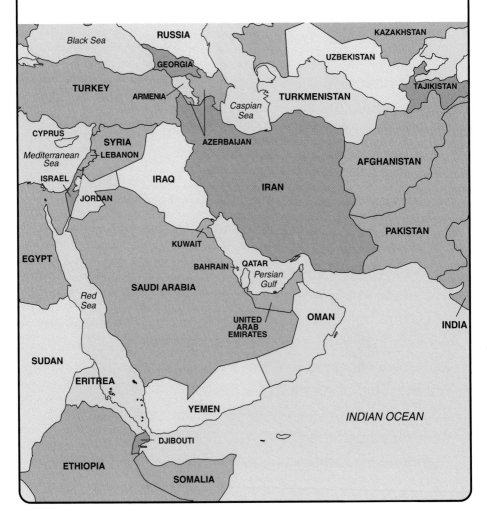

worried that Iraq also might invade their country. So the United States sent its Army into Saudi Arabia to help defend Kuwait. This was known as the Persian Gulf War. After the United States and the United Nations won the war in 1991, American **troops** stayed there to keep peace in the region.

Osama bin Laden had become an Islamic extremist. He didn't like the ideas of the United States. He also considered the land of Saudi Arabia to be **holy** since Muhammad was born and lived there. He was angry with Saudi Arabia for letting the United States Army into the holy places of Islam. He argued with the government of Saudi Arabia. He escaped from that country in 1991 and settled in a country in northern Africa called Sudan. In 1994 Saudi Arabia took away bin Laden's citizenship.

While in Sudan, bin Laden became more and more angry. He began planning terrorist attacks. The United States and other nations began to put pressure on the government of Sudan not to help bin Laden. In 1996 Sudan sent Osama bin Laden out of the country. So bin Laden asked his friends in Afghanistan to allow him back into their country, and they did. Shortly after that, the Taliban took control of Afghanistan. The Taliban called bin Laden a guest and gave him shelter.

Why does bin Laden hate the United States?

Osama bin Laden has given several reasons for hating the United States. The presence of American troops in Saudi Arabia is usually first on his list. Islamic extremists like Osama bin Laden believe that only Muslims should be near the places where Muhammad lived. They want American troops out of the holy lands of Islam. It makes them very angry to think that Americans are living on these lands.

A second reason Osama bin Laden hates the United States involves the country of Israel. Many Jews were killed during World War II. Some people

After the Persian Gulf War, U.S. troops set up housing in Saudi Arabia.

thought Jews needed a country of their own. Israel was created in 1948 as a home for the Jews. The land of Israel was chosen because Jews believe God promised them that land. But both Jews and Muslims were living there.

Land where Israelis and Palestinians live

The Muslims in this area are called Palestinians. The Israelis and Palestinians have fought several wars over this land. There has not been peace in this area since the early 1900s.

Israel has a **democracy** like the United States. The United States often has helped Israel in its war with the Palestinians. This has made Osama bin Laden and other Islamic extremists angry.

A third reason Osama bin Laden hates the United States goes back to the Persian Gulf War. To punish Iraq and to make sure it would not attack again, **sanctions** were placed on Iraq. The United States agreed with these sanctions. This means several countries do not buy Iraq's oil. Iraq makes a lot of money from selling oil. So it does not want to have sanctions against it. Osama bin Laden is angry that these sanctions are hurting the Muslim people of Iraq.

Why is bin Laden a prime suspect?

President George W. Bush called Osama bin Laden a **prime suspect** in the attacks of September 11, 2001. The American government suspected bin Laden because he has been involved in several terrorist attacks against the United States.

One of the first attacks bin Laden might have planned was in 1992 in the country of Yemen. Many people think he also was involved with the first attack on the World Trade Center in 1993. Since then, bin Laden has been accused of planning terrorist attacks against the United States in many countries.

In 1998, members of bin Laden's Al Qaeda bombed two United States **embassies** in Africa. An embassy is a place in one country where officials from another country work. The bombs killed 224 people and hurt more than 4,500 others.

Al Qaeda also is blamed for bombing a United States Navy ship called the USS *Cole* in October 2000. The ship was attacked while stopping for fuel in the country of Yemen. Seventeen American sailors were killed in the terrorist attack.

CHAPTER 4

September 11, 2001

Pennsylvania

Pentagon

World Trade
Center

On September 11, 2001, four planes were hijacked. At 8:45 A.M., the first plane crashed into Tower One of the World Trade Center. At 9:03 A.M., the second plane crashed into Tower Two. Forty minutes later, at 9:43 A.M., the third plane crashed into the southwest side of the Pentagon. At 10:10 A.M., the fourth plane crashed in a field in Pennsylvania. Both World Trade Center towers collapsed. The Pentagon was badly damaged. Nearly 5,000 people died. Citizens from 86 nations were killed in the attacks.

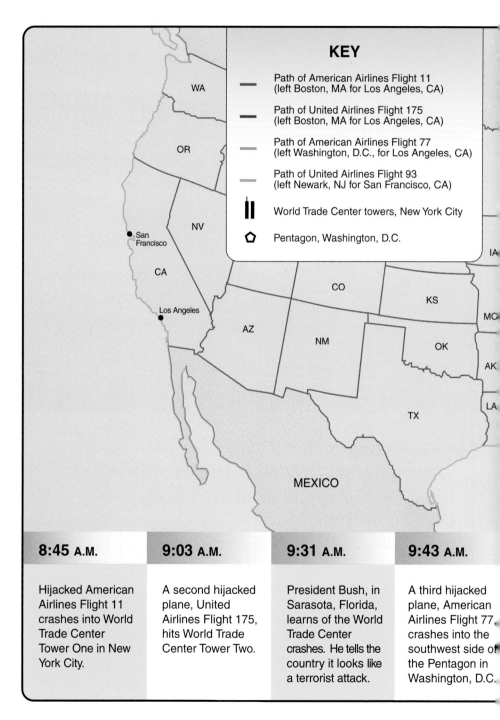

KEY

— Path of American Airlines Flight 11
(left Boston, MA for Los Angeles, CA)

— Path of United Airlines Flight 175
(left Boston, MA for Los Angeles, CA)

— Path of American Airlines Flight 77
(left Washington, D.C., for Los Angeles, CA)

— Path of United Airlines Flight 93
(left Newark, NJ for San Francisco, CA)

‖ World Trade Center towers, New York City

⬠ Pentagon, Washington, D.C.

8:45 A.M.

Hijacked American Airlines Flight 11 crashes into World Trade Center Tower One in New York City.

9:03 A.M.

A second hijacked plane, United Airlines Flight 175, hits World Trade Center Tower Two.

9:31 A.M.

President Bush, in Sarasota, Florida, learns of the World Trade Center crashes. He tells the country it looks like a terrorist attack.

9:43 A.M.

A third hijacked plane, American Airlines Flight 77, crashes into the southwest side of the Pentagon in Washington, D.C.

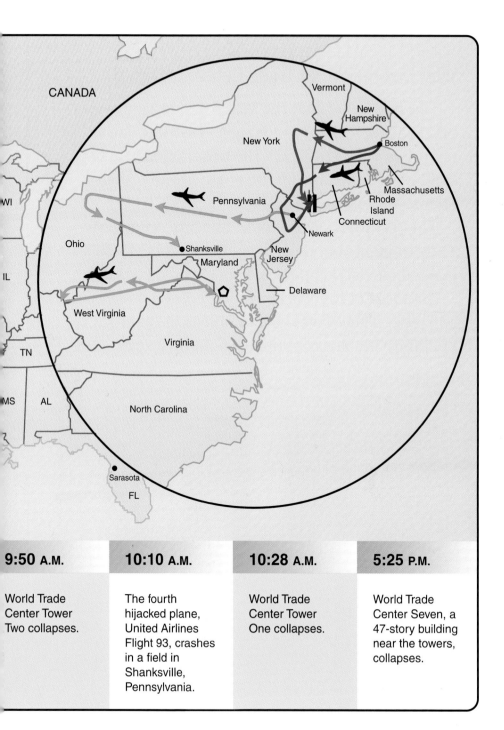

9:50 A.M.	10:10 A.M.	10:28 A.M.	5:25 P.M.
World Trade Center Tower Two collapses.	The fourth hijacked plane, United Airlines Flight 93, crashes in a field in Shanksville, Pennsylvania.	World Trade Center Tower One collapses.	World Trade Center Seven, a 47-story building near the towers, collapses.

Why was the World Trade Center attacked?

You remember that the World Trade Center was part of New York City's Financial District. The terrorists chose to attack the towers because they **symbolized** the financial strength of the United States.

The terrorists also wanted to scare Americans. They thought that destroying the towers would stop many financial companies from doing business.

But most of the World Trade Center workers are still alive. They have opened offices in other buildings and are continuing to do their jobs.

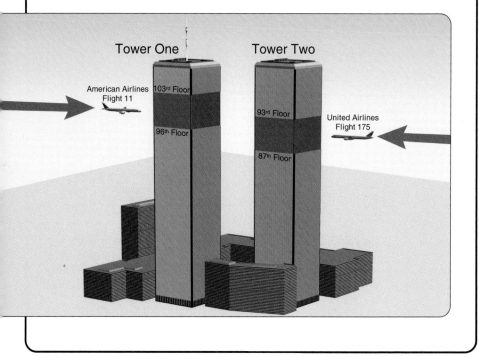

Tower One

Tower Two

American Airlines
Flight 11

103rd Floor

96th Floor

93rd Floor

87th Floor

United Airlines
Flight 175

Why did the towers collapse?

On the morning of September 11, 2001, millions of people watched their televisions as the events unfolded. When the planes hit the towers, there were huge **explosions**. Even with flames and smoke blowing out of the huge holes in the buildings, few people thought that the towers would actually collapse.

The fuel inside the planes, known as **jet fuel**, caught fire. Jet fuel burns at a much higher temperature than regular fire. And unlike some other fires, water will not put it out. The fire actually floats above water. The jet fuel burned at nearly 1500°F, hot enough to bend the steel in the buildings. The part of the buildings that was above the planes was too heavy for the melting steel to support. But it was more than the weight that made the buildings collapse.

When the top part of the towers fell, it created movement. The bottom floors of the towers had always been able to support the full weight of the towers. But when the weight of the towers was falling, the speed and movement created force. The force pushed down one floor on top of another all the way to the bottom. Think of a hammer resting on your foot. The weight of the hammer does not hurt your foot. But if you dropped the hammer on your foot, it would hurt. The movement gives the hammer more force.

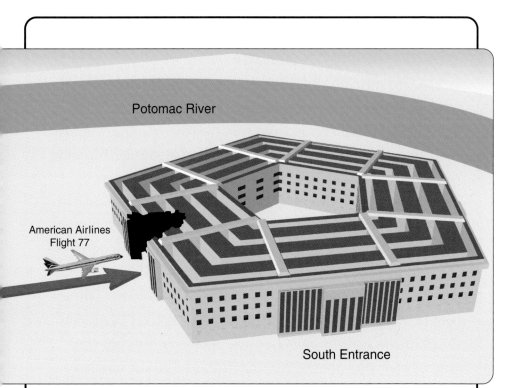

Potomac River

American Airlines
Flight 77

South Entrance

Why was the Pentagon attacked?

Just as the World Trade Center was a symbol of America's financial strength, the Pentagon is a symbol of America's military strength. The terrorists wanted to scare people. They thought that by destroying the Pentagon, Americans would be afraid that the government couldn't defend itself against an attack.

But the terrorists did not destroy the entire Pentagon. Remember that the Pentagon is made of five rings. The plane crashed through three of these rings. But only a small part of the building actually collapsed. People were able to return to work in the Pentagon building within weeks after the attack. In fact, the part of the building that the plane hit had just been rebuilt and improved. Stronger steel and stronger windows kept the plane from doing more damage.

What happened on the Pennsylvania flight?

One of the four hijacked planes did not crash into a building. Instead, it crashed in a field in Pennsylvania. When the plane was hijacked, many of the passengers began calling their families from phones on the plane. Some of these families had been watching television and could tell the passengers about the World Trade Center and the Pentagon.

Once the passengers learned this information, they knew they had to do something. Several passengers planned to fight the hijackers and gain control of the plane. The struggle resulted in the plane crashing in Pennsylvania. Some believe that the hijackers on this plane were trying to crash the plane into the White House or the Capitol.

By crashing into a field, the plane did not kill any more people on the ground. It did not destroy any more American buildings.

Who were the heroes of September 11, 2001?

The heroes of September 11, 2001, were all the people who risked their lives to help others. The passengers of the Pennsylvania flight were heroes. They fought the hijackers even though it was dangerous. Other heroes were inside the World Trade Center and the Pentagon. One man died because he would not leave his friend who was in a wheelchair.

The New York City **firefighters** were also heroes of September 11, 2001. When the first plane hit the towers, hundreds of firefighters went inside to help people. They climbed up the stairs into the weak buildings to bring people out. When the towers collapsed, many of the firefighters were still inside helping people. More than 300 firefighters and police officers died that day. More firefighters died that day than in the 50 years before.

How has America responded to the attacks?

Life changed for all Americans on September 11, 2001. Many people knew someone who died in the attacks. Some people became afraid. But Americans felt closer to one another than ever before. Within hours after the attacks, the American flag started showing up on cars, houses, and clothes. This love for one's country is known as **patriotism**.

People gave a great deal of money to the families hurt by the attacks. They also gave blood to help the people injured in the attacks. President Bush asked every American child to **donate** one dollar to help the children in Afghanistan. Millions of people have thanked firefighters for the hard work they do. President Bush asked the United States Congress to declare a war on terrorism. He said the United States would fight against terrorists and countries that help them.

The government searched for all people involved in the hijackings. Airports looked for better ways to keep people safe.

The terrorist attacks did make Americans sad and angry about the thousands of people who died that day. But the attacks failed in many ways. Most of the people escaped from the World Trade Center before it collapsed. The Pentagon was hit at its strongest point and where the fewest people were. All four planes were less than half full. The United States **survived** the attacks and has become stronger. It will protect its freedom. It will never forget the people who died on September 11, 2001.

In Their Own Words

"Anybody know what that smoke is in Lower Manhattan?"
—Pilot flying over New York City at 8:50 A.M.

"Today, our fellow citizens, our way of life, our very freedom came under attack."
—George W. Bush, President of the United States of America

"I looked up. There was a fireball coming out of the building. I dropped my bag and just started running."
—Sonya Fernandez, one block away from Tower One

"We were completely shocked. It's unbelievable, unbelievable, unbelievable."
—Yasser Arafat, Leader of a Palestinian group

"I was on the phone talking to someone in the building when it happened. He said, '. . . the whole building just shook,' and then I could hear screams. I don't know what happened to him."
—Witness working near the towers

"We can only imagine the terror…and the many, many…people who have lost their lives."
—Tony Blair, Prime Minister of Great Britain

"We had a lady in front of me, who was backing up and screaming, 'Everybody go back, go back, they've hit the Pentagon.'"
—Mike Walker, on a road in front of the Pentagon

"Tomorrow is another day. New York is still here, and we will rebuild and be stronger than ever."
—Rudy Giuliani, New York City Mayor

Glossary

collapsed (kuh lapsd) Collapsed means fell down in pieces.

construction (kuhn STRUHK shuhn) Construction means the act of building things, such as houses or roads.

democracy (duh MAHK ruh see) A democracy is a type of government in which the people vote for their leaders.

donate (DOH nayt) To donate is to give something for an important cause.

drought (drowt) A drought is a long time without rain.

embassies (EHM buh sees) Embassies are places in countries in which officials from other countries and their staff work.

entertainment (EHN tuhr TAYN mehnt) Entertainment is music, dancing, movies, television, and other ways people enjoy themselves.

explosions (ek SPLOH zhuhns) Explosions are very loud bursts.

financial (feye NAN shuhl) Financial means having to do with money.

firefighters (FEYER FEYE tuhrs) Firefighters are people whose job is to fight and put out fires.

hijacked (HEYE jakd) Hijacked means stole by force. Some terrorists have hijacked airplanes, buses, or boats.

holy (HOH lee) Holy means very important to a religion. Something that is holy is considered to be very pure and free from evil.

independent (IHN dee PEHN duhnt) Independent means free from another's rule.

injured (IHN juhrd) Injured means hurt.

invaded (ihn VAYD ihd) Invaded means entered with force in order to take control.

invest (ihn VEHST) To invest is to buy stock, or parts of a company, in hopes of making more money.

investment firms (ihn VEHST mehnt FUHRMS) Investment firms are companies that help people buy and sell shares of stock.

Islamic extremists (ihs LAH mihk ehk STREEM ihsts) Islamic extremists are Muslims who believe that the Koran tells them to fight other people. They believe that all people who do not practice Islam are evil.

jet fuel (JEHT fyool) Jet fuel is a liquid that is needed to make an airplane's engines run.

Koran (koh RAN) The Koran is the most important and holy book of the religion Islam.

landfill (LAND fihl) Landfill is trash and other materials used as soil.

military (MIHL uh TEHR ee) The military is the soldiers and officers who fight in case of war.

patriotism (PAY tree uh TIHZ uhm) Patriotism is a feeling of love and pride for one's country.

pentagon (PEHN tuh gahn) A regular pentagon is a closed figure with five equal sides and five equal angles.

prime suspect (PREYEM SUHS pekt) A prime suspect is the person who others believe most likely did a crime.

observation deck (AHB suhr VAY shuhn DEHK) An observation deck is an area at the top of a tall building. From the deck people can see far away.

religions (reh LIHJ uhns) Religions are beliefs in a god or gods and teachings for how to live.

rugged (RUHG ihd) Rugged means rough.

sanctions (SAYNK shuhns) Sanctions are acts done by a group of nations in order to force another nation to do or to stop doing something. One sanction might be that the nation is kept from shipping goods.

severely (suh VEER lee) Severely means in a very serious or mean way.

skyscrapers (SKEYE skray puhrs) Skyscrapers are very tall buildings with many floors.

stock market (STAHK MAHR keht) The stock market is a place where parts of a company, called shares of stock, are bought and sold.

strict (strihkt) Strict rules are rules that must be followed exactly. If people break these rules, they will probably be punished.

suicide bombers (SOO ih seyed BAHM uhrs) Suicide bombers are people who are willing to kill themselves in order to kill large numbers of their enemy.

survived (suhr VEYEVD) Survived means continued to live after a terrible event.

sway (sway) To sway is to move back and forth.

symbolized (SIHM boh LEYEZD) Symbolized means stood for, or represented.

terrorism (TEHR uhr IHZ uhm) Terrorism is the act of using force or threats to scare people or a government into doing something.

terrorists (TEHR uhr ihsts) Terrorists are people who try to scare other people or a government into doing something. Terrorists might hurt or kill people, or they might say they will do so.

troops (troops) Troops are soldiers.

Index